Mrs. Zukie's
Doodles
Coloring Book
A sweet, Adorable, Kawaii book
with chibi character to color

This book belongs to

ISBN: Softcover 978-1-5434-8311-6
eBook 978-1-5434-8379-6

Rev. date: 02/21/2018

FART

Hi

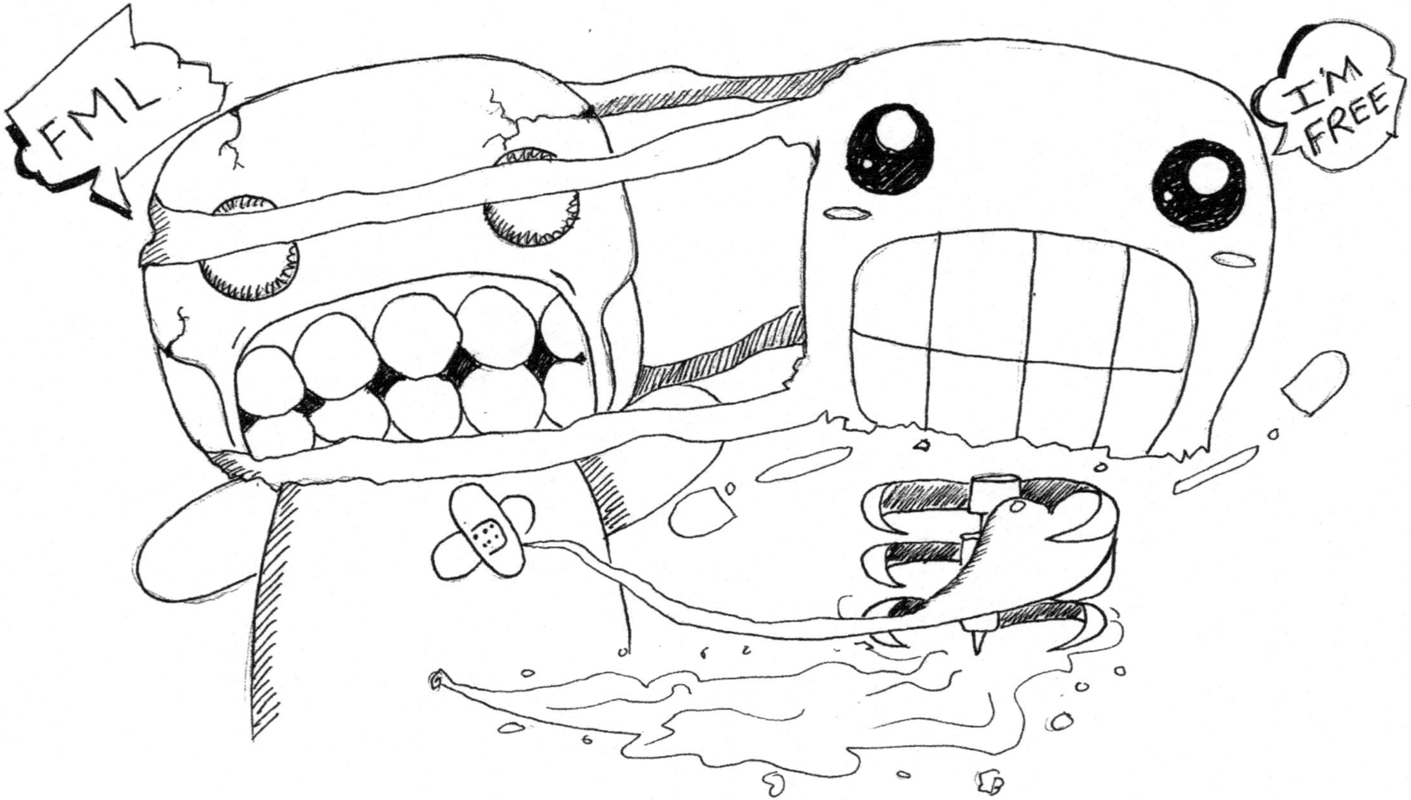
FML
I'M FREE

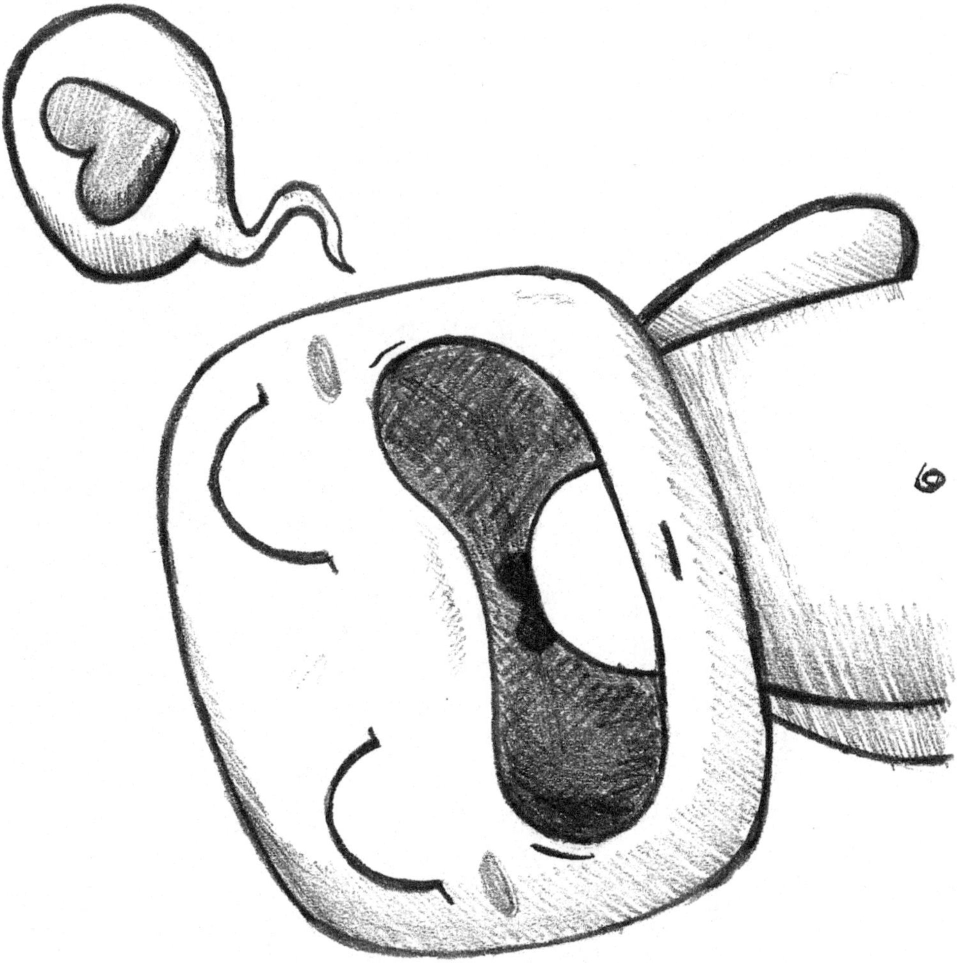

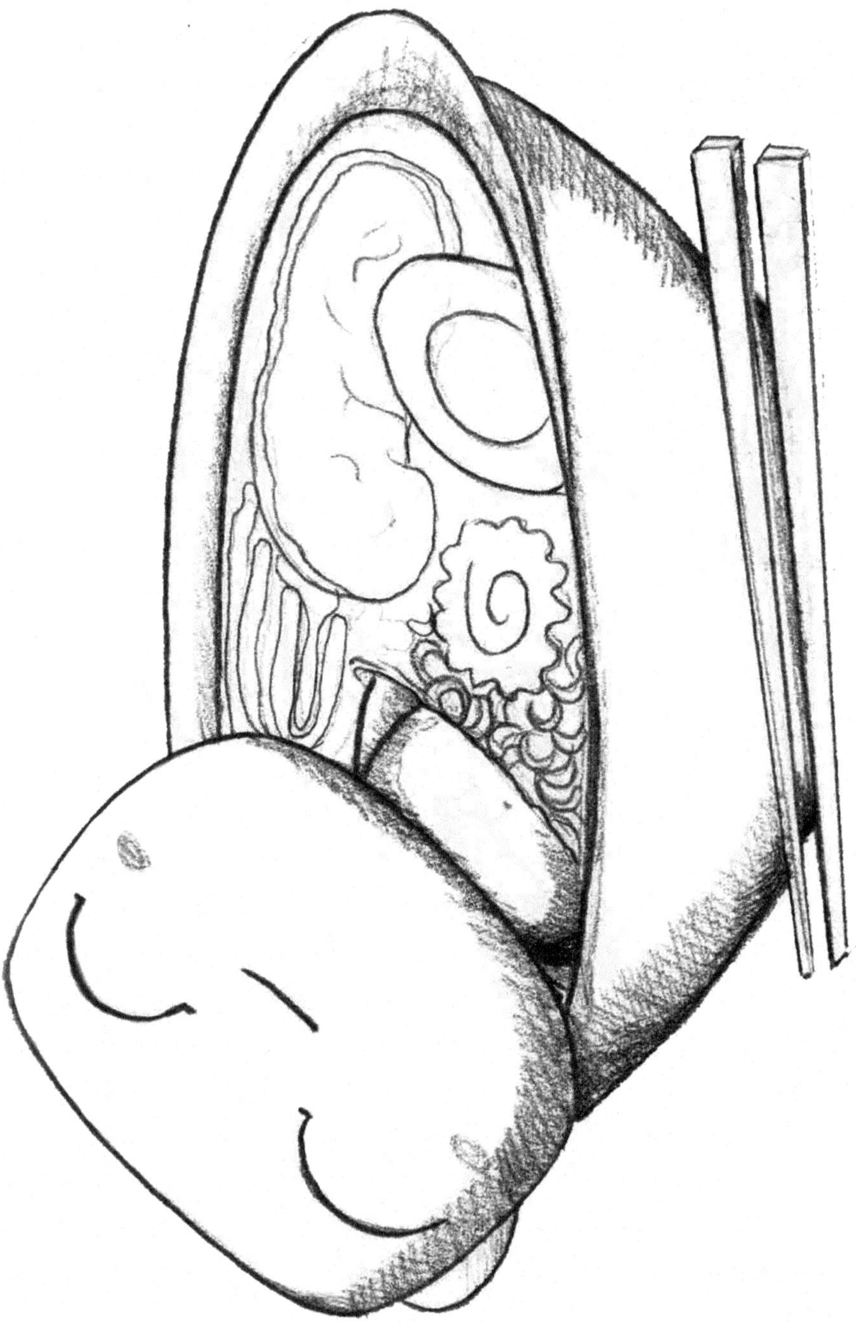

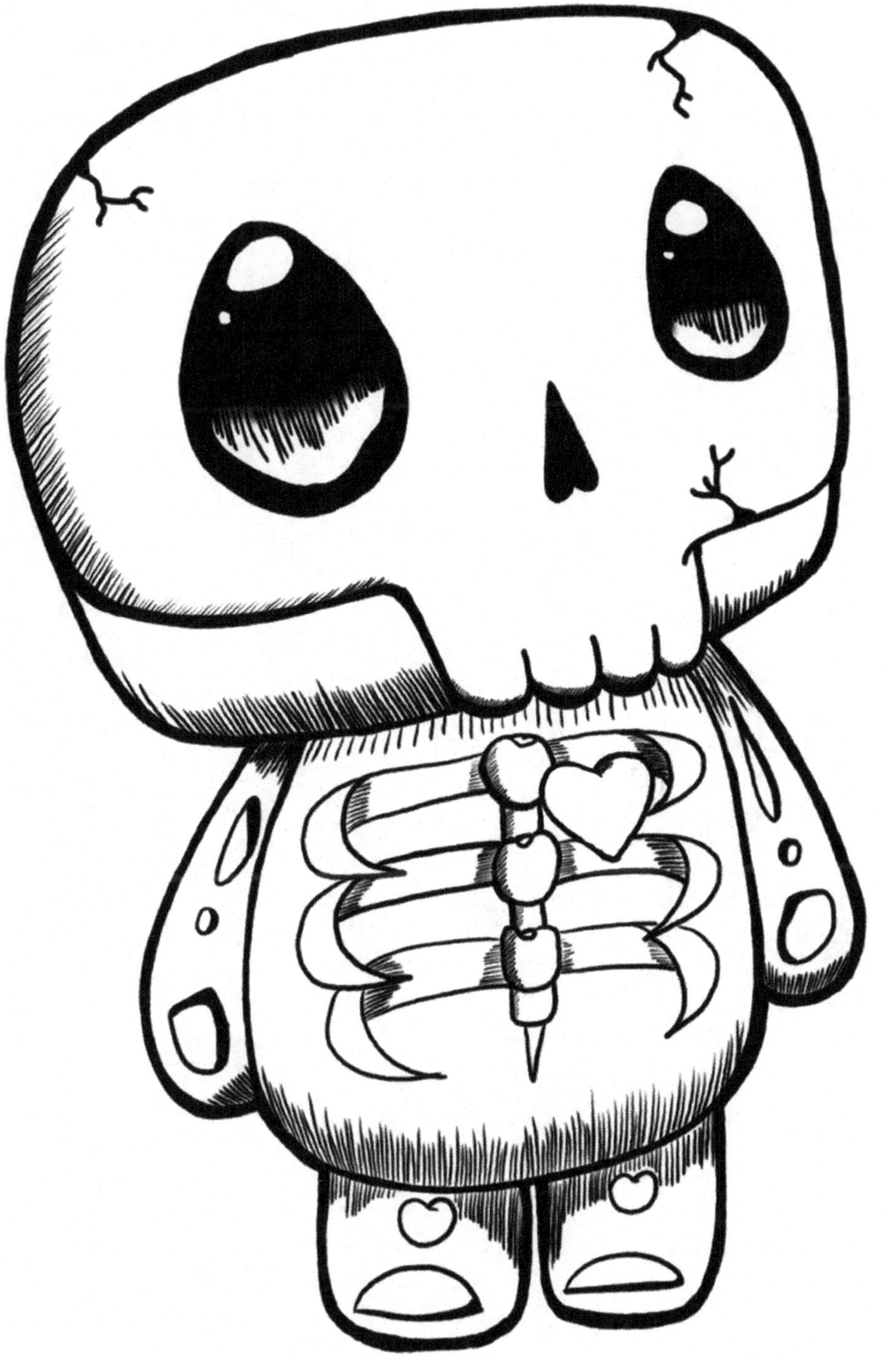

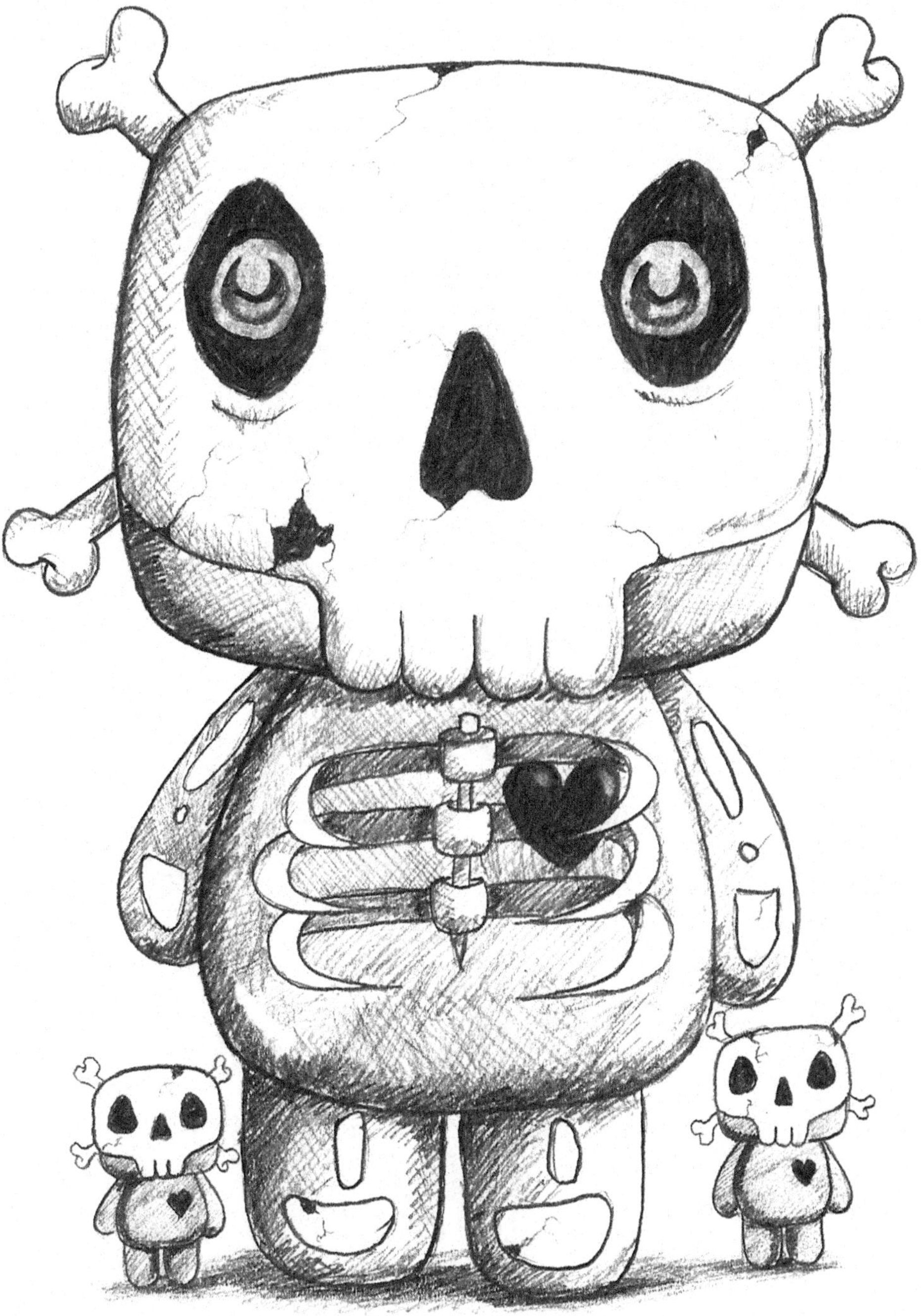

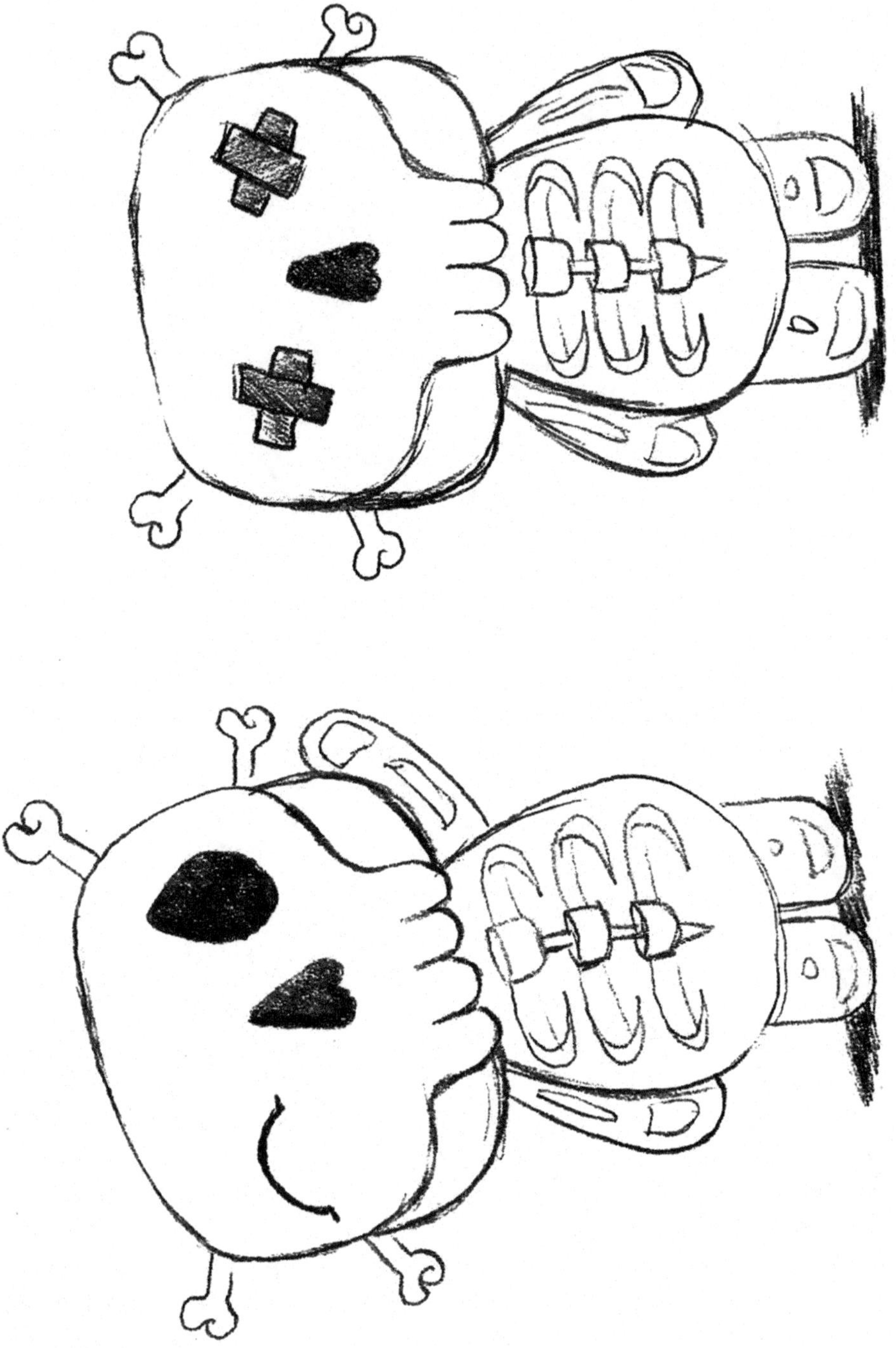

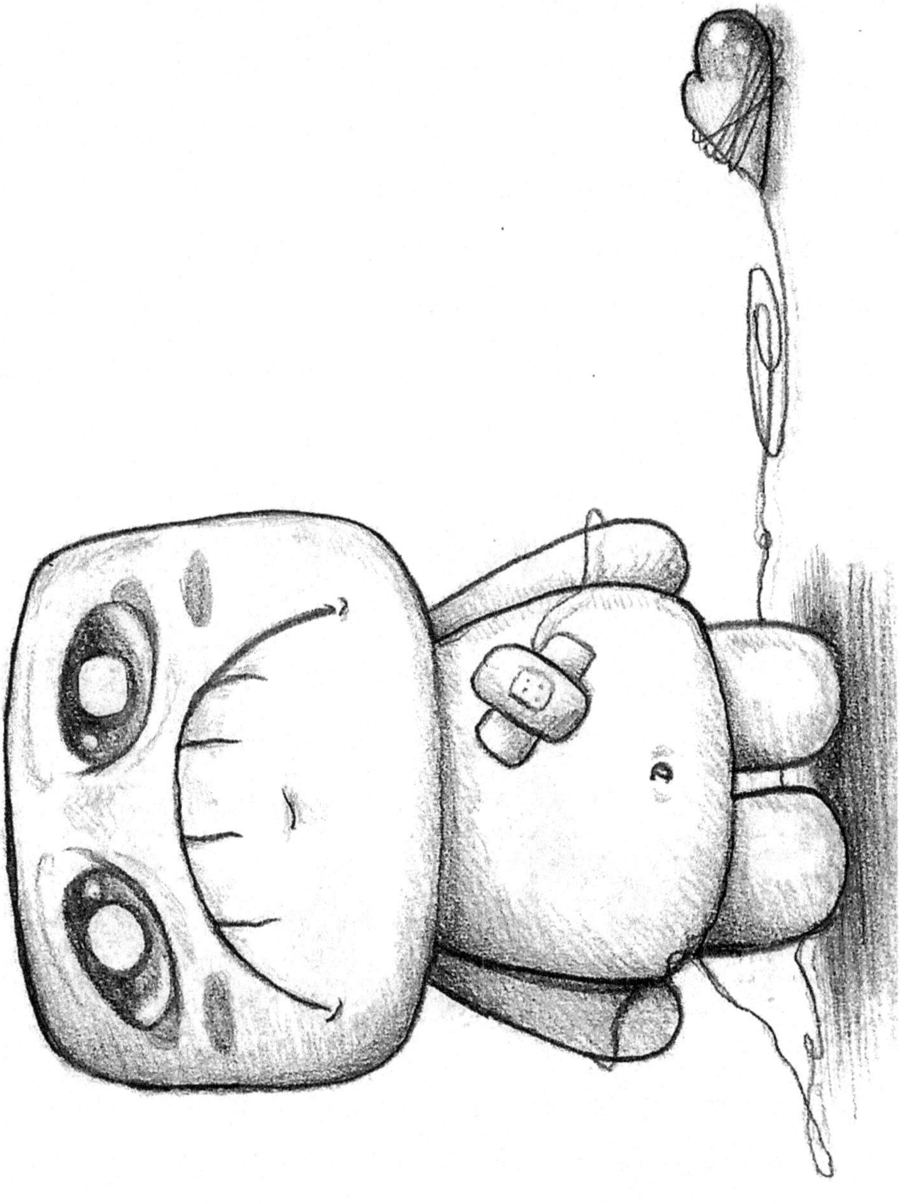

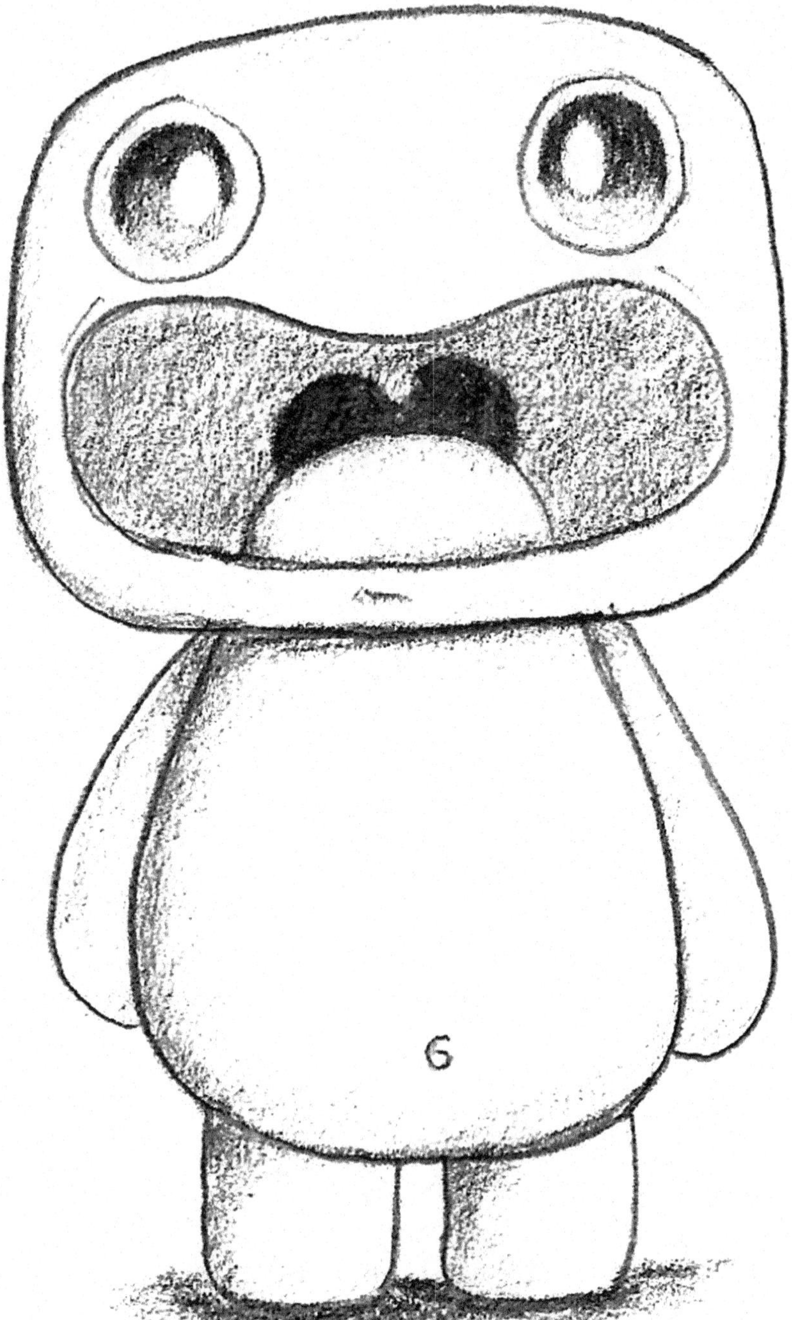
6

Printed in the United States
By Bookmasters